PLAIN

PLAIN

CONTEMPORARY
SMART SELLING

Victor Femi-Fred

ISBN-13:9781721750214

Published in Nigeria by
Ventra Consult
21, Ajanaku Street, Awuse Estate,
Off Opebi Street, Ikeja, Lagos, Nigeria
+234-8035203397

hhtp: //ventraconsult.com
email address: information@ventraconsult.com
email address: victorff@ventraconsult.com;
victorfemifred@yahoo.com

Printed in Nigeria by:
Bengraphics Publishing House
+234-81734278
bengraphics07@yahoo.com

CONTENTS

ACKNOWLEDGMENTS

I have been blessed to have the help and support of many to whom I want to express my sincere thanks and appreciation. I thank the Good Lord for all, my life, health, job and my travels. Thank you Jesus, I love you so much.

I thank my beautiful, loving and hardworking wife Fadeke Femi-Fred, who still does not know I love her so much. Without her support and her love, I am so sure I won't be where I have found myself today. Thank you eternally sweetheart, I so love you.

My children, Victor Junior and my daughter Princess Stephany, who I always look at with so much admiration and pride knowing I owe them a better tomorrow as their father. I love you both so much. You both are my joy.

My parents: HRH. Late Anthony Alao Femi-Fred Iyelafe II and Olori Mrs. Victoria Alao Femi-Fred; Dr. M. O. Omidiji who always encourages and inspires me; my trustee, Mrs. E. O. Omidiji (the best mother in-law in the whole wide world); My best uncle (who inspires me daily with his persona of fairness and uprightness) Hon. Justice of the Federal High Court of Nigeria, Justice Nathaniel Emmanuel; my eldest Sister, Mrs. Anthonia Olorunmonu; My K. E. M. I. Mrs. Kemi Olowoake; T. I. T. I. Mrs. Titilope Okuyiga; Late Miss Edith Alao (May Her soul RIP) and, Mrs. Francisca Poopola. Charles Alao, my brother who challenged me always. Biodun Omidiji, Oscar Okuyiga, my Chairman, Olaolu Okuyiga, Rev. Fr. Francis Mario, Anthony Alao Femi-Fred Junior, my favourite aunt in-law, Dekanla Sanyaolu, my favourite brother in-law Olalekan Sanyaolu (RIP). Olawale Sanyaolu. Dr. and Mrs Olaosebekan, Uncle Lasiele, Abdulrasak Ibrahim, Laide Temowo, you have always been by me with your prayers all through, you will always have that space.

To my global mentor Felix Binggeli, who showed me the ropes of becoming a globally certified sales & learning facilitator (Thank you). Daniel Cox (my role model), the energetic facilitator/negotiator with a difference. Peter Lemmens another mentor of mine, Dave Jenkins, Suleiman Shaik (my brother from another mother), Michelle Johnstone (whose MEA Learning Leadership gave me a purpose), Ela Altinpinar, Vuyolwethu Somhlahlo, Mayokun Aduwo, Azza Hassan, Dennis Smit, Oluwatoyin Adejumo, Charbel K. Bou-Eid and Antoine Bridi (my godfather).

Mrs. Hafsat Bello, my guardian who took me in her arms and pointed me to a career in sales. I owe you so much. Hon. Justice Mrs. Funke Anuwe, you were there for me in my early days struggling to understand life as a seller.

Dr. Lemmy Omoyinmi, another role model of mine who, despite his busy itinerary, always finds time to encourage me and also sacrificed his time to edit this book for me. Thank you Uncle Lemmy. Uncle Lasun Omidiji, thank you for your words with their banters.

And finally to so many individuals who have in their own way either knowingly or unknowingly contributed to the creation of this book. Demola Adeyemo, Karis Kehmi, Jude Emiyede, Ola Yusuf Amoo, Angela Iwunze, Tunde Alimi, Olumide Ariyibi. Yemi Ogunade, Tope Raphael Ojo, Fabian Wellignton.

A very special thank you must also go to my editor Nath Mc Abraham-Inajoh, the Principal Partner of Mc Abraham's Limited (a CMD Certified Management Training Institution). He was in charge of training for four and half years as the General Manager of the Federal Airports Authority of Nigeria, (FAAN). He holds both the Bachelor and Master's Degrees in English Language and an MBA in Management, majoring in Human Resource Management and a member of both the Nigerian Institute of Management (Chartered) and the Chartered Institute of Personnel Management of Nigeria.

He has been involved with lots of training and consultancy services.

Thank you Nath for all the inconveniences I caused you with this book.

<u>PREFACE</u>

I have had the privilege of travelling this great world for almost a decade sharing with sellers across the globe on how to be a better and a more effective seller in this modern age of ours.

There is nothing like the passion derived from the closure of a sale and more significantly a complex multi-dimensional sale. That bell being rung in the office is overwhelming every time it goes off. More so, the thought of meeting the expectation of thousands of people with just a deal closure is always so satisfying and fulfilling.

Then comes the sales commission that confirms a job well done. Such a great feeling of satisfaction.

One of the things I have long shared with my delegates all over the world has always been: understanding the client is not all rocket science but the application of both "arts" (the finesse and the persona used to explore the understanding of the client's needs) as well as the "science" (methodology applied to complete the sales cycle from the understanding phase through the satisfaction phase at the end leaving no dissonance).

All through my travels, I have noticed the same knowledge gap for sellers across the globe irrespective of the background or regions, thus the urge to add my voice to how to become a more efficient seller.

This book ensures a basic understanding of the requirements for success using basic contemporary concepts at achieving sales success.

Understanding the modern-day buyer and becoming an effective seller requires quite a tremendous effort with simplicity and methodology following global best practices as shared in this book, amongst other books.

DEDICATION

This book is dedicated to all sellers who are challenged on how to be successful in their sales career. In today's marketplace, the success of sellers lies only in the basics of Sales. "Contemporary Smart Selling".

Victor Femi-Fred
'2018

FOREWORD

In reading this book, I have come to appreciate the more the basics of sales and the simplicity with which the author has put them in different perspectives. Most importantly, I have come to understand and acknowledge that today's buyer has changed. Thus; the need for sellers to act and be different.

Jill Konrath says: "by turning yourself into the primary differentiator" a seller can still stand out from the competition. Most complex sales deals happen with eye contacts and handshakes which, most often than not, earn the required trust.

Sellers must understand that sales success is all about the mindset. The right mindset is needed to mitigate all the uncertainties that come with the changing buying behaviours of the clients.

You simply must be determined and ready to succeed through skilling up with the right tools/methods which are the basics as highlighted in this book.

This book shared how best to focus on "contemporary selling" to adapt with experiences shared from other subject matter experts on how to become more successful as a modern-day seller.

Identification of the need for constant learning and its adaptation to new methods/strategies by the seller towards gaining the competitive advantage is very important and well-articulated in this book.

A seller must always identify what prevents sales from happening. It is not only by "working hard, but by working smart".

Dr. Lemmy Omoyinmi
Director with VISION Development Nigeria.
African Regional Trainer for the
International Trade Center (ITC),
an initiative of the UN, Geneva.

INTRODUCTION

In today's ever-changing marketplace, sellers are faced with dealing with knowledgeable buyers who want trust, integrity and speed of response. This want has necessitated a change in the dynamics of today's seller with questions on how equipped they are to surmount these major communication and engagement challenge.

This gap has therefore urged me to share my cents' thoughts through this book on how to address some of these modern-day seller's challenges.

This book is aimed at sharing the basics of smart selling in today market implementing contemporary sales methods that help address the communication /engagement gap mentioned above between today's buyers and today's sellers.

The definition of contemporary "is existing at the same time or of the present time period". This book aims to align with the selling concepts required to be successful in todays' marketplace where we have smart buyers.

In the book "Contemporary Selling" (Building

Relationship, Creating Value) by Mark W. Johnston and Greg W. Marshall, both who "created a comprehensive, holistic source of information about the selling function in modern organizations that links the process of selling (what sellers do) lends credence to the required focus for a review of modern methods of selling. They believe that customer relationship management, social media and technology-enabled selling, and sales analytics continues to set the standard for the most up-to-date selling in the market today." Going further, they both attested to laying emphasis on the client. They shared the importance of focus on securing and building a long term relationship mutually that is beneficial with today's buyers.

I believe that the success of selling requires not only a good understanding of the buyer, but most importantly back end preparation to know the buyer. This requires knowing the buyer through research on his personality, profile, industry, organisation and its environment. I also, from first-hand experience, believe that every buyer today wants a seller with the business mind-set towards earning trust. A very good example is the use of social media tools such as LinkedIn, Twitter, Facebook etc. these have provided the means to research target buyers, understand their preference, personality prior to engaging them. These social media tools are used to research buyers for better understanding prior to engagements.

No matter what you are selling, buyers' value becomes relative and requires the right method to be unveiled through contemporary methods as expressed in this book.

Today's sellers are most often than not embroiled in price as value, when most of the time, it is not. These are the challenges faced by today's sellers. This book thus highlights how best to identify these buyers values.

Sellers, are therefore looking for ways to combat these modern-day buyers' challenges which lead to continuously trying to answer questions such as: "What best strategies, tactics or tools do they practice/share with sales teams when enlightening them on how to be effective sellers?" Sellers are also questioning whether it is important for them to become more knowledgeable on clients or on offerings with challenging varying responses to these questions. In my opinion, this again requires a volunteer that will steer the sellers in the right direction with the appropriate answers... and that can only be a leader. This leader will be charged with the responsibility of better articulating and coordinating the sales thought process.

Myles Munroe in his book, Becoming a Leader, said: "A

good leader not only knows where he is going but can inspire others to go with him" to buttress the need for a sales strategy. I also agree that sales leaders should inspire and help sellers improve. However on the other hand there is a major difference between sales leadership and sales management. Sales leaders empower their sales team to succeed. In one of my job roles as a seller my managing director, taught me how to schedule meeting time with my clients, knowing the best time to go meet with them. Learning the timing of the executives helped me a lot during my direct selling days. It has helped shaped my daily client meeting scheduled. As a result, the sales leader is the person who leads the sales organization to generate predictable and repeatable revenue for the company.

On the other hand, the sellers are expected to conduct research through varying resources available to bring themselves up to speed on the requirements and peculiarities needed to be successful at identifying these values that buyers crave for. It is understood that modern day buyers follow very closely industry trends to understand what their competitors are doing and how they are doing them so they can keep pace. It thus becomes imperative that the sellers also follow their target industry to bring themselves up to speed as well.

Therefore, it is within these dynamics that we must

accept and face the challenge of identifying the differentiator to become a sales professional within the confines of global best practices. Knowing full well that what we call "selling" is really the act of finding what interests people and how best to speedily respond to these interests. This is what this book tries to share with you, the reader.

CHAPTER 1

WHAT IS SELLING?

Selling is to give or hand over (something) in exchange for something. It is to persuade someone to accept, convince someone of the merits of, talk someone into, bring someone around to, win someone over to, get acceptance for, win approval for, get support for something. Thus, selling in today's market place is seen as first and foremost a transaction between the seller and the prospective buyer or buyers (the target market) where money (or something considered to have monetary value) is exchanged for goods or services.

Imagine what would happen to the business you work for if it had no sales? It probably wouldn't stay open for very long! If no one ever patronize an organization, it would most likely closeup shop eventually. And if no one bought the goods a factory produced, its days would be numbered. This is one thing every business has in common goods and services must be sold in order for businesses to exist.

Selling is a marketing function that involves determining client needs/wants and responding through planned, personalized communication that influences purchase decisions while enhancing future business opportunities. Because selling is planned and personalized, it goes beyond mere order taking or client service. Let's see the different determinants for successful selling:

1.   Selling is about communication. Without effective communication, there is no understanding and this leads to a breakdown in exchange, because the art of selling is so dependent on persuasive and believable information exchange, sellers must be effective communicators. Great communication is not simply   what is conveyed, but how it is conveyed and how choice   rhetoric, info and body language can drive relationships and sales.

2.   Selling adds utility. Utility in this case could also be usefulness of offerings (could be product or services), through selling, offerings can be "in the right place at the right time." Skilled sellers aid in developing utility for their offerings by creating client desire. Selling enables clients to receive help with their buying problems. In this way, clients can determine   their needs and can select offerings that are right for them.

3.   Selling Creates desires. Desire for offerings is

what leads to an actual sales intent. Skilled sellers are required to create such desires for new or established offerings. They do this by determining clients' needs, wants, and buying motives. Then, sellers explain offerings features, advantages and benefits to clients to further heighten today's buyers' desires. Since you understand the company's buying motives, you would be sure to focus on the time-saving benefits of your offering in your sales presentation. This is professionally understood to be the "compelling reason for the client to act now".

4.   Selling helps others determine needs. By providing opportunities for two-way communication between buyers and sellers, sellers enable buyers to receive help with their buying problems. In this way, buyers can determine their needs and can select offerings that are right for them. Sellers should be able to recognize the importance of correctly identifying clients' needs; ask the right questions to accurately identify needs; identify and take advantage of cross-selling opportunities.

Goods and services are sold for ultimate consumption. Business-to-consumer (B2C) is business or transactions conducted directly between a company and consumers who are the end users of its products or services. The business-to-consumer as a business model differs significantly from the business-to-business model: Business-to-business refers to commerce between two or more businesses. These two types of business models help attest to the bottom line that selling plays a key role in our society and economy. It can occur anywhere be it tangible or intangible, to consumers directly or indirectly even if through the middlemen called intermediaries.

The selling concept holds that consumers and businesses, if left alone, will ordinarily not buy enough of the selling company's offerings. Therefore, organizations must undertake an aggressive selling effort to be successful as enumerated below:

1.   Selling skills. There are specific selling techniques that have been proven over time to be more effective. As you become more skilled and advanced in selling, you will learn how to:

- Determine buyers' needs, wants, and buying motives
- Suggest additional or substitute items
- Demonstrate offerings
- Follow up on Sales
- Open, Progress and Close Sales

- Question buyers professionally
- Handle buyers' Objections as appropriate.

A seller for example, can ask a prospect, "Is it OK to ask a few questions about your business and then I will share the value of how our offerings can help address some the business challenges you might be facing. There might just be a potential fit for both of us?" this approach allows the buyer to feel comfortable and understand what is coming next. This also allows the seller to open up a two-way street in the selling process so that both you and the buyer get to a win-win conclusion.

2. Belief in selling as a service. In other words, selling is a service. Your focus should be on the buyer and what the buyer wants. What you can offer the buyer? How can you help the buyer? You aren't there to make a quick buck or "arm twist" a buyer into buying something the buyer doesn't really need. Your job is to assist buyers by giving them the accurate information/guidance they need to make intelligent buying decisions. Think of yourself as the go between for your business and your buyers. By meeting the needs of your buyers, you will be helping your company and yourself grow and prosper.

3. Communication skills. Good communication skills are handy in every industry, but they are especially important in sellers' career. You must be able to express yourself clearly and simply so that buyer understand how your offerings will benefit and meet their needs. Remember that good communication isn't a one-way street. You must be sure to pause for breath regularly practising the "Talk & Listen" (Professionally known as the 80/20 rule). This means you talk ONLY 20% and listen 80% as you actively listen to your buyer! In sales how, you say things to a buyer matters more than what you say, sellers need to speak clearly, not too quietly, and not in a monotone. Sellers need to let their emotion and personality shine through during sales engagement. According to Sandler Sales Training, only 7% of communication relies on the content of what you say, whereas 38% of communication is about other attributes of communication. Good communication depends on your ability to observe your surroundings.

4. Creativity. Successful sellers don't rely on the same old tricks every time they interact with a buyer. Use your imagination and look for new or

improved uses   for your offerings! Listen carefully to the buyer and personalize your sales pitch based on their needs. But if you know that a certain business values quality over   all else, you might change your pitch around to focus on the reliability of the offerings. Good sellers are able to think on their feet and you can do that as well. If you want to know more about your buyer, take advantage of the social media tools such as LinkedIn, Facebook, etc.

5.   Personal appearance. I am sure you will be used to the saying "first impression lasts long". Remember you only have one shot to make a first impression. Buyers judge you and your organisation mostly that first time from the way you dress and groom yourself. If you present yourself as dishevelled and sloppy, the buyer will assume you and your company does business in the same manner. Think about it this way: would you be comfortable while at a hospital if you see a doctor, for the first time, in a T shirt and Jeans when you are   used to seeing doctors in corporate formal wears with the white overall? Just think about this and reflect, then you will understand why your appearance means a lot to selling. Pay attention to appearance standards in your industry and dress appropriately.

Therefore applying "Contemporary Smart Selling" methods, we need to take a holistic view which means that we are interested in engaging and developing the whole process of selling.

You can think of this as different levels, physical, emotional, mental and spiritual. It aligns with the concept that the human being is multi-dimensional.

This is based on the development, design and processes that recognise end to end of selling. Vince Lombardi said *"Winning is a habit, unfortunately so is losing."* Thus, once you learn what selling is, it then becomes a habit. *"Habit is habit and it's not to be flung out of the window by any man, but coaxed downstairs a step at a time"*, so says Mark Twain.

In today's marketplace of continuous change and perceived offering parity, sellers are the key differentiators, thus the need for todays' sellers to learn and refresh with "Contemporary Smart Selling". It is the major contributor to sales success today. "Contemporary Smart Selling" success requires change that guarantees success, knowing that the only constant thing in life is change and more change.

     # TODAY'S BUYERS

As the focus of buying control has changed, the very character of buying has been transformed. Much of the frustration felt by the traditional seller results because today's buyers are more sophisticated, skeptical and self-contained than ever before.

Today's buyers therefore require agile and iterative reaction from the sellers. According to Ray Collins and John O. Gorman in their book "the buying revolution" there is a new manifesto for the buying revolution with the obvious truths with budgets being slashed, managers finding themselves in strait-jackets thinking about the what, when and how they can buy. They also noted in truth that buyers are more than ever being self-contained which has led them to be more structured, strategic and skilled in their approach to major purchases.

They confirmed that managers are increasingly playing it safe and deferring decisions to the most senior levels. These new buyers think that sellers who do not have the following attributes can evidently not meet their needs which in turn has led to the need to have sellers become agile in their approach using contemporary concepts and methods. So what are those attributes that has become a "no no" to buyers? Here we highlight the focus for a successful engagement with today's buyers :

- TALKS TOO MUCH
- DOESN'T LISTEN
- PUSHY
- FALSE/INSINCERE
- PROVES TO BE KNOW IT ALL OR SHOWING OFF
- RUDE AND WITH BAD MANNERS
- UNPREPARED
- LACKS OFFERING/INDUSTRY TRENDS
- NOT PUNCTUAL
- INTERRUPTIONS
- FINALLY NOT TRUSTWORTHY

The reality is that today's buyers have learned not to trust a typical seller who always engages in the propaganda of just selling in the form of a generic value statement. They are always with the YES answer to all questions thrown at them. Today's buyers believe that sellers are too careless with their promises, always making promises they can't meet up with.

Today's buyers are wary that sellers are always making the same universal claims which lead buyers to conclude that sellers always respond the same way.

This shows that the seller has not differentiated himself/herself from the competition.

The speed at which sellers arrive at solutions after just the first meeting often results in questions about the level of understanding of the buyer's needs.

Finally, sellers often continually use crude and manipulative/traditional sales techniques. This attributes often portrays the "good cop, bad cop" negotiating ploy. This is always hilarious.

It has become so obvious that today's buyers are far more educated especially within the B2B (Business-to-Business) industries. This education is also extending to the B2C (Business-to-Consumers) space as well. Chicago Tribune also attested to these claims that more research continues to demonstrate the education of buyers. For example, the CEB's sales research suggests that 57 percent of buying decisions are made before any calls are placed to potential solution providers (sellers).

DemandGen in another survey, revealed 77 percent of B2B buyers did not speak with any sellers until after they had self-educated themselves. The education weapon of choice today is the internet.

To work with the educated buyer requires a potentially different marketing approach. Content marketing through blogs to even LinkedIn Pulse helps to demonstrate your knowledge and trust as a key solution provider.

As buyers become more educated, they are seeking different sales conversations. They want to see sellers articulate the value of their solution. Unfortunately, more research from Sirius Decision stated that, for the last four years executives believed only 34 percent of the sellers they encountered could articulate value.

For all those in the businesses marketplace, value articulation may begin within digital selling using such as the LinkedIn profile. If the LinkedIn summary does not highlight the value to connect with you, then you are potentially missing many sales opportunities.

Probably the greatest impact of educated buyers is the inability to convert sales leads. Forrester's sales research suggests 99 percent of sales leads do not convert while LinkedIn has a sales conversion figure at 87 percent.

When we remember people have always bought from people they know and trust, then we may be able to appreciate educated buyers and not work against them.

This appreciation is also a reflection of our emotional intelligence.

The educated buyer is more your friend than your enemy. Of course, there will always be tired kickers and price hagglers and they are not your ideal buyer.

Find your ideal buyer, build long-term relationships with them, respect them and further educate them. You will become their trusted authority, which is far more beneficial than being their trusted adviser.

Another school of thought with Mike Renahan identified what today's buyers look out for in today's buyers. Sellers know what they want in a buyer. Sellers spend hours searching LinkedIn using specific keywords, titles, and more to identify perfect fit buyer. Then, their outreach campaign begins.

But what most sellers forget about, is what the buyers considers as value. Sales is about relationships, so both sides need to be equally engaged.

Before a seller can begin reaching out, they need to understand what today's buyer's values are. Here are five things modern buyers value above all else.

1.   Content

The information gap that once gave sellers an edge over the buyer no longer exists. Buyers now have access to offering information, pricing details, research, and more all at the click of a button. In fact, today's buyer goes through nearly 60% of the sales   process before they even talk to a seller.

But just because buyers can get content without the help of a seller doesn't mean sellers can't facilitate the research process. Because buyers put a significant emphasis on content, consider sending a helpful piece of collateral to buyers, or even creating a blog post or case study.

A study conducted by Eccolo Media found that the two most important pieces of content to B2B buyers were white papers and case studies. Of the survey, 48% of respondents said case studies were "very" or "extremely" influential in their purchasing decision.

2.   Reviews

Sales used to be built on what the seller told the buyer about the offering. Now, buyers conduct their own research, and use buyer reviews - what others say about the offering - in their buying decision.

Reviews play a major role in the sales funnel. In fact, according to a Bright local Survey, 88% of respondents said they consulted a review prior to making a purchasing decision.

The reviews, however, go beyond the offering. What a buyer thinks of the seller herself also has bearing on buying decisions. A study by Nielsen found that buyers are four times more likely to buy when referred by a friend. And those referred buyers have a lifetime value that's 16% higher than non-referred buyers. That's a lot of money for the seller and the business. I have witnessed sellers move from one organisation to another with their buyers moving with them. I am an example of this.

3. **Passion**

Passion might be the most underrated tool on a seller's belt, especially in B2B sales. A passionate seller is one who's going to stand by their buyer and work twice as hard to ensure that the buyer succeeds.

Clients love passionate sellers because their passion is contagious, according to Erin Murphy of the University of Pennsylvania. Passion wears off on the person they are talking to, and in turn, makes them more passionate about what they are pursuing. It's a tremendous effect.

But what does passion look like? As Mark Hunter writes, *"Passion in sales is evident when the seller takes the time to listen to their buyer and attempts to really understand what it is they are looking for. It is displayed not only in the questions that are asked, but also in the tone of voice and body language the seller uses and the follow-up demonstrated after the sales call."*

To demonstrate passion, go beyond the sale and check in frequently. The best sellers know their buyer's ongoing success is just as important as their own. By touching base frequently and ensuring that everything is going smoothly they can showcase how interested they are in their buyer.

4.   Ability to listen

In order to truly understand a buyer's objectives/

pain/challenges/goals and vision, sellers must listen. Buyers value sellers who listen to them, ask the right questions, and strive to solve their specific needs. According to Dave Warawa, listening is the most important form of influence during the sales process.

This reminds me also of Felix Binggeli (IBM Global Sales School Learning Leader for Growth Markets, my mentor whom I am very fond of). He always shared the concept and principle of listening as 80/20. He says: a seller who talks more will miss "hooks" an example, *the buyer says in his opening "it's going to be an hectic half year with all the project we are thinking about..."the seller if not listening actively will not hear this and continue the conversation. The ideal would have been asking questions from the cues e.g. "what types of projects, what initiatives are generating these projects, what impact does half year have on the projects etc".* These missing cues thus gives more room for doubt rather than confidence with the buyer. I personally believe having two ears means it should be applied in equal proportion to only one mouth that we have.

Felix shared with me often, how to target

questioning towards achieving results and also listening afterwards with rapt attention. He suggested always using follow up questions on initiatives, objectives, timelines, project team members, next steps towards project completion, potential expected ROI, with key performance indicators etc., *an example, the buyer responds with importance of completing a project within a time frame..." the seller should ask follow up question such as "what happens if this is not achieved with the projected timeline, what are the expected reward during this projected timeline or question could be, how much impact will missing the timeline have on the business... etc"* He always highlighted that this type of questioning will expose the "why, how and priorities" on the issues discussed. He also emphasised that "qualifying and quantifying" questions will help sellers uncover the financial metrics behind buyers objectives/issues/challenges such that these financial impacts will drive the buyer to an instant understanding that will in turn generate a reaction. These reactions could show the urgency for a resolution required to address the business challenge of the buyer. Another type of questioning he shared with me includes "leading and collaborative" questioning that challenges the buyers into thinking what would change if they respond to the purchase.

This influences the buyer towards a decision. The final type of questioning he shared with me was to always have confirmation questions that will cause the buyer to reflect on all discussed towards achieving a mutual agreement required to progress the sales. Usually these questions are closed questions with a simple "yes or no" response. These learnings from Felix always stuck with me and now I share them with my readers.

To corroborate what Felix Binggeli always shared on listening, Dave Warawa offers an articulated simple, but powerful strategy for improved listening skills. He's very clear; he believes that effective listening isn't simply about remaining quiet, it's about working to gain a deeper understanding of what other people are communicating. Here are his five success principles that can improve your listening skills today:

Ask powerful questions - The person who asks powerful questions, learns a great deal from the buyer.   Most People buy based on their feelings.

To consider a powerful question, there are no right or wrong, but it must be applicable in the context of the engagement.

A powerful question builds from the situation, so what's powerful in one instance might not be in another. A good example could be during a conversation with a decision maker who is currently challenged on budget, the question "what will be the impact of the discussed initiative(s) challenge on business if not addressed" can in this case be considered as powerful. On the other hand, asking "do you have budget" can also be considered, but if o u t   o f context, then it loses the power intended. It is often said that children ask an average of 400 questions in a day, while adults only asks 6 questions. Your thoughts on why is as good as mine.

- They justify based on facts. Keep these two formulas in mind:

  . The seller's questions should incorporate powerful questions and paraphrasing.

Potential importance of powerful questions are inclusive of aiding your buyers' curiosity, triggering a reaction and unveiling a potential opportunity during the discussion among many others. Powerful questions are well now for stimulating reactions.

All these come into context when the contemporary seller is in the know that today's buyers' goal is to obtain goods and services that meet their needs and wants. Buyers are faced with varying problems associated with acquiring offerings to satisfy these needs and wants while they make specific types of decisions in order to obtain desired goods and services.

- Actively listen - Don't just listen to your buyer – hear them! Too many sellers listen for a break in the conversation to make their point. Don't interrupt. Gain understanding of the person's feelings by considering this equation:

  - 100% of all talking = 75% from the client + 25% the seller
  - 100% of all listening = 75% the seller + 25% the client
  - Feelings = Words Used + Emotions Expressed

- Paraphrase - Repeat back to the client what you heard him say in your words, not his. Start your paraphrase with, "So if I understand you correctly..." or "Let's see if I'm on the right track...." Successful paraphrasing requires you to actively listen to the answers to the great questions you asked.

.   Successful paraphrasing = clarity of understanding

- Summarize the Client's Needs - Provide a verbal summary of all of the client's needs in a full statement. When you do so, watch for the smile and nod...you are gaining rapport, respect and trust - the key ingredients in building the strong relationship required to complete a sale.

- Personality Projection - This is not rocket science nor open heart surgery. We are communicating. Smile, have fun and enjoy the journey to best understanding your client's needs. People like people who like people. Get it? The more people you like, the more people like you. People will always buy from people.

5.   Honesty

The question on buyer's mind would be."Would you rather buy from a sleazy smooth-talker, or someone who's up front about who they are and what they do"? It's a no-brainer.

The honest seller doesn't try to persuade a buyer one way or the other. They simply offer information to clients throughout the sales process, and facilitate the buyer's decision. Your best bet is to throw away the script, and simply solve for the client.

Word it is said travels fast, and never more so than in today's marketplace, where social media has become cultural. Given the challenges that exists in today's marketplace, it is crucial to stay conscious about how we want to be known individually. Never over-promise on capabilities or costs, even if it means you may not win the deal. In the long-run, this approach will pay off, and there will always be another opportunity.

The modern buyer values new things, and the modern seller needs to adjust accordingly. The relationship between these two continues to evolve. For now, a seller needs to have excellent content, strong reviews, and a few key traits to be successful.

While facilitating a sales training earlier this year in

Dubai, UAE, I heard a seller who shared a success story on how honesty earned her respect with her client which eventually translated in repeat business. She made an honest mistake of over One Hundred Thousand dollars in the contract she only just signed with the wrong scope of work. On discovery with her team, she went back to the client to explain and share with transparency the errors. To her dismay, the client understood and appreciated the honesty even though the client knew from value offering comparison with competition, that there was an error. They both revisited the contract and amended as appropriate ending with a "win-win". Another seller could have done otherwise leading to mis trust upon delivery.

I personally think it's time to rethink how you're approaching your clients. A field that was once built on seller holding all the power has b e c o m e one that is focused on the buyer. Today's buyer has just as much information as the seller and doesn't need to go to them for much other than to actually purchase the offering or to seek clarification. It is therefore up to y o u to adjust accordingly.

In this new era of the empowered and informed

buyer, traditional sales strategies are becoming less and less effective. Cold calling and "show up and throw up"are fading into the sales twilight while warm outreach and relationship building moves to the forefront. Instead of hard selling, modern sellers need to start developing and using new sales techniques that are both good for the buyer, and good for the seller. Here are five sales tactics that sellers must embrace to remain relevant.

a. Modern sellers Don't Sell, They Help

Thanks to the internet, buyers no longer need to rely on sellers for basic offering information, and this drastically changes the role of the seller in the buying process. High-pressure sales tactics no longer work on informed clients who are more than capable of gathering data and making their own decisions. So what's a seller to do? Prioritize helping over selling.

Modern sellers help their clients by answering questions, brainstorming solutions to pressing problems, and offering clarification about their service or offering. If a buyer wants to know the differences between their offering and a competitor's, helpful sellers answer honestly and enable the buyer to better understand the relative merits of each option.

Helping also means being there when it comes to support issues. Some sellers might hand the problem off to another team member after the deal is inked, but helpful sellers stand by their clients' sides through the thick and thin. If the client isn't delighted with their purchase, inbound sellers work hard to solve the problem.

Here are five questions to ask next time you're speaking with a buyer to make it clear you're committed to helping them above all else:

i.   Is there any part of the offering you found confusing and would like clarification on?
ii.   How can I help you decide whether or not this offering is for you?
iii. What kind of value do you want to see out of this offering?
iv.   What can I do to help you better understand our service?

v. What are the major challenges you're grappling with, and how can I help you solve them?

b. Modern sellers Build Long-Term Relationships, Not Short-Term Sales

In the past, once a buyer signed on the dotted line, the seller would often vanish (until the time came to renew the contract).

The modern-day seller has a different approach altogether. Developing a relationship with clients is critical in today's sales environment. As author Ken Cook puts it: *"Relationships matter because selling today has evolved. Twenty-first century sales success depends on trust before solutions."*

And the relationship has to start from day one. The old sales play book advocates for trying to build a connection out of thin air with cold calls. But consider that 64% of sellers say cold calling has not improved in the last three years. The modern inbound sellers research their clients, engage with them online, and seek warm introductions to build rapport - before they ever pick up the phone. After the relationship is forged, then and only then is it time to introduce the buyer to their offering.

Here are three easy ways to build a relationship with a buyer:

1.   Engage with them on social media. Whether it's LinkedIn, Twitter, or Facebook, sparking up a conversation and becoming familiar to a buyer is an easy way to foster a connection.

2.   Ask a ton of questions. Get to know your buyer. Ask questions that go beyond the usual "How's business?" Dive into family, sports, the weather, interests, passions, goals -- any and all topics that might help you build a relationship.

3.   Follow up often. By sending a "Hey, how are you?" email every two or three weeks, you'll start to develop a personal bond with your buyer. Not only is communicating regularly a great way to build rapport, it will also help you stay top of mind with buyers.

c. Modern Sellers Sell Strategies, Not Offerings

Clients have overarching plans and goals for their businesses, and as a seller, it's your job to help them achieve these objectives. In other words, a modern seller isn't just the "offering guy," they're also business strategists.

Solving for the buyer and/or client is the most important part of being a seller today. Instead of dumping an offering into buyers' laps, offer them strategy advice to help them achieve their goals. Approach every buyer as if they could become your next great case study.

The best way to help with development and strategy is to learn where your buyer is at both on a business and personal level today and where they want to go. It's important to ask open-ended questions here and give your buyer a chance to candidly speak to their challenges, goals, and dreams.

A few easy ways to assist with strategy:

1. Analyze the buyer's market and look for

opportunities for improvement.

2. Share content and case studies of companies that experienced success with new tactics, and ask for buyers' feedback.

3. Hop on the phone for regular check-ins to ensure they are staying the course and getting to where they want to go.

d. Modern Sellers Are Authentic, Not Scripted

Cold calling with a one-size-fits all script in hand is no longer an effective method for building a relationship. Buyers now expect personalization and customization in all their interactions.

Gaining trust is critical in building rapport with today's buyers, and the best way to do that is to be genuine from the get-go. In fact, Brian Tracy says that a seller's unique personality can be responsible for up to 80% of their success.

The easiest thing to do to start embracing

your personality is simple:

Throw away the script.

By researching your clients, creating tailored decks, and getting rid of the generic sales script every other seller on the floor is using, you'll allow your personality to shine through. Don't miss your chance to go a little off the grid and connect with clients on a personal level, and not just a business level.

e. Modern Sellers Issue Guidance, Not Demands

Inbound sellers should take time to discover what their buyers need and genuinely care about. It is important that buyers' goals and challenges are identified as this shows that sellers are not focused on simply forcing an offering down buyers' throats. Instead, the modern-day seller shows believe in providing guidance and options to every buyer to ensure that they are getting what's best for their buyers business.

As HubSpot's VP of Sales, Pete Caputa said: sellers should "give more than they receive."

On your next sales call, put together a list of three options for your buyer. The first one might be your offering, the second a competitor, and the third the status quo. Objectively discuss the pros and cons of each decision and how it could affect business in the long term. Instead of bragging about your offering, present all the choices the buyer has, build trust, and then let them make a decision.

f. Modern Sellers Are Inbound, Not Outbound

While outbound sellers cling to outdated and no longer effective cold sales tactics, inbound sellers are adopting the above behaviors to better serve the modern buyer. Rather than automating obtrusive sales tactics of old, inbound sellers are revolutionizing the way they sell.

The inbound seller has all of these new tactics in their back pocket. They're focused on being themselves with every buyer, offering help, building long-lasting relationships, assisting with strategy, and offering guidance and options as each buyer

CHAPTER 3

HOW TO BECOME AN AGILE SELLER

In our engagement with businesses and clients we recognize that solutions become relevant when they solve real business issues and help clients become more efficient and agile. The key to success is connection and I personally believe very strongly in the importance of working in chunks to strengthen the interaction between the sellers and the buyers. It is through connection that we accomplish our goal of delivering solutions that provide client value and satisfaction.

I have mentioned the importance of communication to understand the clients' needs and challenges, using listening and questioning. I shall be taking a look at the tools required to make all these come together.

Buying Behaviour; understanding client's concept of features, advantages and benefits; understand industry trends/analysis; understand the importance of feedbacks, etc.

1. Client's Buying Behaviours

Buying behaviour is the behaviour that buyers

display while searching for offerings that they expect will satisfy their needs. It is the decision processes and actions of people involved in buying and using offerings. It also refer to the decision-making process used by clients regarding market transactions before, during, and after the purchase of either a good or service. It is usually seen as a particular form of a cost–benefit analysis in the presence of multiple alternatives.

Let's look at an example based upon buying a new smart cell phone. The first stage is likely to be that the buyer has a need for communication or access to the Internet, or faced with the challenge he cannot interact with friends using social media. The value added by products such as Android, iPhone or Windows phone and others should satisfy the buyers needs or solve the concern. So the second stage is where the buyer speaks to other people and surfing the Internet looking at alternatives gathering information on the best product to purchase, which represent stage two. The buyer might visit a local cell phone store to speak to the sales staff to complete stage three, i.e. buyers evaluation of alternatives. Stage four   will be the selection of final choice from the alternatives. The final stage, stage five involves the buyer's post-purchase evaluation whereby the use of the phone having a positive or negative experience of the product. If the purchase doesn't satisfy the buyer's needs the buyer will take an action and more importantly the buyer tell others of the challenges with the purchase choice, but If otherwise pleased with the product, the buyer will tell others and this will influence stage two (their information search process) when others decide to buy a cell phone.

A well-developed and tested model of buyer behaviour is known as the stimulus-response model which is well discussed by Philip Kotler, who also belongs to the school of thought of those who identified the different stages of the consumer buying process. It thus becomes imperative that contemporary sellers understand this new trend and integrate it into their process to achieve success. They are Need Recognition, Information Search, Evaluation of Alternatives, Purchase and Post Purchase Behaviour.

It is however very important to note that as an agile seller, you must strive to create an enabler for repeat business and not to create a dissonance. Dissonance, which is buyer's remorse, usually stems from unhappiness after post sales. This decision arises when a person has had to take a difficult decision with huge investments, but resulting in unsatisfied feelings.

To be agile does not mean changing your sales approach, but to adapt to the ever changing market place in which we have found ourselves. Worthy of note is that buyers have changed fundamentally, drastically, and for good. They don't need you anymore. When they have an issue, they go online to research their problem. They check multitudes of web sites, looking for information that can help them understand their challenges, how others are solving it, opinions on best solutions, and more. They download white papers, attend online events, read articles, listen to audios, and check out forums. In short, buyers self-educate, leaving the seller totally out of the loop. When they finally decide to engage, they're often 60 – 70% of the way through their buying process! It's only when they know what they want that they call in the sellers for final decision making. Here's the good news: what today's buyers are demanding is not impossible. Every single seller is capable of doing what's necessary. When you do, you get radically different responses.

According to the Aberdeen Group, sellers who leveraged online resources to learn about clients saw revenue jump over 21 percent. In CEB's studies, sellers who challenged clients' thinking and brought them fresh insights significantly outperformed their colleagues. These findings show that engaged and knowledgeable sellers clearly have an important place in today's marketplace. Buyers' expectations have changed, sellers need to understand clients' value drivers. Drivers that will drive the clients to a decision making position, drivers that will influence decision making process and finally drivers that will impact on the buyers decisions.

If all these are well articulated, then it becomes imperative that contemporary sellers are on track to becoming more agile, knowing the answers to What they buy, Why they buy, When they buy, Where they buy, How often they buy, How they use what they buy and How often they use the purchase. Research on buyers has been better described by Dr. Brian Monger (CEO of MAANZ International and a Professional marketer and consultant with over 40 years' experience). In his presentation titled "Introduction to Buyer Behaviour" he highlighted types of buyers Interpretivists and Positivists. The Interpretivist

This essentially provides data for strategic managerial decisions.

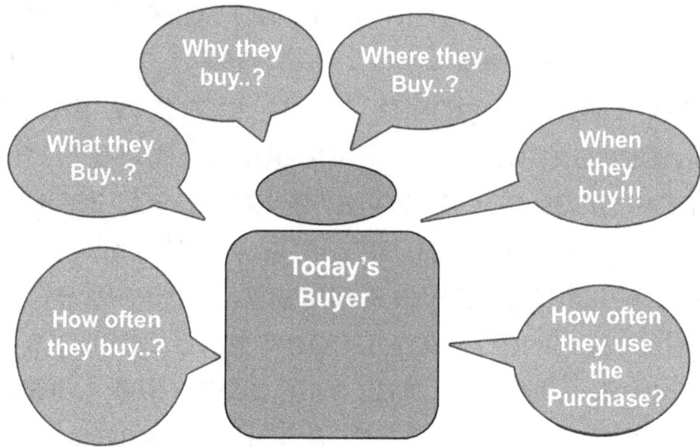

Fig. 1. Buyers Decisions to make.

It is however, quite important to understand that these buying behaviours can be affected by the following three factors: Personal, Psychological and Social.

Personal buying behaviour usually refers to target clients with unique personalities. They thus focus on determinants such as demography, i.e. sex, race or age etc. These determinants are considered as major influencers in their decision making.

Secondly, Psychological buying behaviour is seen as the motive of the buyer.

A motive is an internal energizing force that orients a person's activities toward satisfying a need or achieving a goal, while actions are effected by a set of motives, not just one. If sellers can identify the buyer's motives then they can better develop selling a mix. However, it should be remembered that the elements in the MASLOW hierarchy of needs are: Physiological, Safety, Love and Belonging, Esteem and Self Actualization. Therefore I urge the readers of this book to determine what level of the hierarchy the clients are at; so as to determine what motivates their purchases.

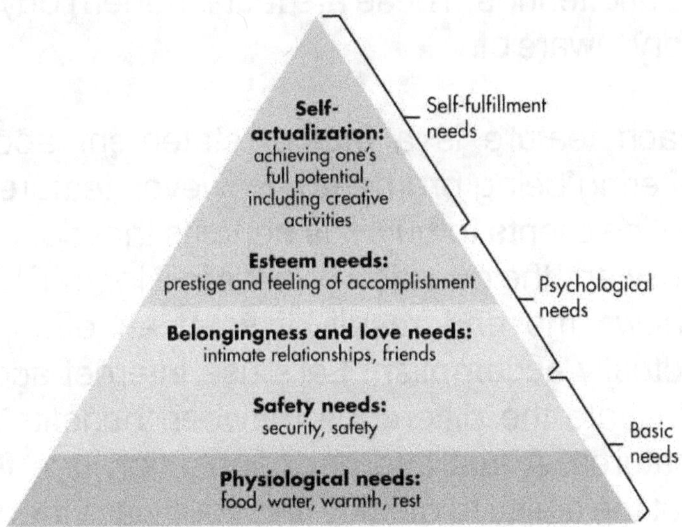

Fig. 2. MASLOW Hierarchy of Need (Courtesy google)

Finally, Social factors. Clients' wants and motives are understandably influenced by opinion leaders, reference groups, industry and culture.

Therefore there is every need to pay attention to these factors if you are to achieve success.

2.   Features, Advantages and Benefits (FAB)

A FAB Statement is explaining the feature, what it does (the advantage), and how that benefits the buyer. Features are one of the easiest things to identify. They are the surface statements about your offerings. These are facts modern buyers are very aware of.

Each feature is a factual statement about the offering being promoted. However, features don't entice clients to buy. It is benefits that do. Benefits answers the question "What's in it for me?" Benefit shows the end result of what an offering can actually accomplish. Let's use internet access to illustrate the difference between benefits versus features. A fast internet connection is a feature, but the ability to quickly find your way when you're lost is a benefit. Features are defined as surface statements about your offerings, such as what it can do, physical appearance etc. I urge my readers not to confuse either a feature or a benefit with an advantage. Advantages are like the intermediary between features and benefits. They are effectively what the feature does to eventually result in a benefit. Still using the internet example, a 4G internet connection (feature) means that you can access web applications in a shorter amount of time (advantage). An example of a benefit could be the use of GPS to help easily find your way home when you're lost. Be sure to make the distinction and understand the relationship between features, advantages and benefits.

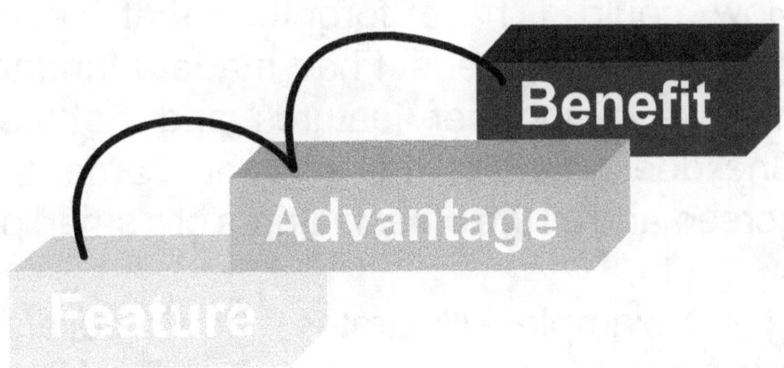

Fig. 3. FAB Hierarchy

In a nutshell, the FAB concept helps explore the features, advantages, and benefits of an offering. With each owning a set of attributes and traits which differs, depending on the offerings at stake and the client in question. Features generally are obvious, but not the benefits.

I remember sometimes back, buying my mother a phone without considering her needs, but mine. I bought her a smartphone and she asked me "what is this Victor?" I replied a phone with all you need, and she laughed at me saying all she needed was just a phone that allows her talk to us her children and also to send short messages. Nothing more". I laughed at myself and remembered what I had always shared, "it is not about you (the seller), but the client (the buyer)".

As sellers how often do we make this mistake? How could I have forgotten that her needs where not my needs. I had made a fundamental mistake giving her features and not benefits. She doesn't need the internet, camera, touch screen and all the other features of a smart phone.

This example illustrates how sellers can misunderstand the attributes of FAB during buyers' engagement process. I therefore suggest that sellers understand the FAB of their offerings and thus address the buyers' needs based on this understanding.

3. Industry Trends

Our marketplace today is ever changing at an unprecedented pace. It is imperative to constantly review your strategy and look at the major trends shaping different industries. That way you navigate the challenges and seize opportunities as they come. To become agile seller, it is important to understand and be knowledgeable about Industry trends. Industry trends are examined to make predictions. They are studies that include trends related to consumer behaviour, technological advancements, new offering development, competition, and other factors that impact the industry in question. It is a market assessment tool designed to provide a business with an idea of the complexity of a particular industry. Industry analysis involves reviewing the economic, political and market factors that influence the way the industry operates and develops.

From a technical perspective, trends involve looking at the statistical analysis of historical data over a selected time frame and charting the progression. A market trend is anything a company does to alter the market in their favour, while market trend analysis is understood to be the analysis of market trends necessary for companies to stay current. Marketing analysis always looks at buyers closely to gauge interest in their product. We can therefore say a market trend is a perceived tendency of markets to move in particular direction over time.

I believe that market analysis, should define the industries that businesses belongs to, the major characteristics of those industries and her major existing players. As a seller, you should understand how you will be able to compete with those industry strengths and improve on their weaknesses.

These trends are classified as secular for long time frames, primary for medium time frames, and secondary for short time frames. Businesses of all sizes use this kind of data to help make informed decisions that will go a long way in improving the business in line with the current trends in the market place. It is very important to understand the difference between Industry trend and Industry analysis. Industry analysis is a business function completed by business owners and other individuals to assess the current business environment. This analysis helps businesses understand various economic pieces of the marketplace and how these various pieces may be used to gain a competitive advantage thus shaping and helping make strategic decisions.

In April 2012, Nigerian government introduced a new policy on cash based transactions which stipulates a cash handling charge on a daily cash withdrawals that exceed NGN 500,000.00 for individuals & NGN 3,000,000.00 for the corporate bodies. This policy obviously will leave an impact on the financial institutions that would require additional infrastructures to support this new policy. With this opportunity in the financial industry, I coached and mentored a seller close a banking front end business process deal worth 6.8million USD with a leading financial institution in Nigeria.

Looking across industries, not only at your own, allows you to see performance trends and assess potential market opportunities. By analysing current industry trends, you could more confidently point your business in a new direction and possibly save it from entering a poor market. Lacy Jo Donald in her publication dated December 6th, 2013 illustrated the need to be informed about trends in industry with a simple nail analogy during her pedicure at a nail salon for a wedding.

Industry analysis is critical for any business professional looking to stay competitive. Whether we're using it to gauge the competition or track our own progress, we regularly monitor our own performance. If you're considering expanding, or

repositioning, your target client base, industry information is an extremely valuable tool to assess the health of different industries. The same industry information you use to gauge your performance, could easily be used to gauge the performance of other industries; allowing you to more accurately note the pitfalls and strengths across sectors and thereby provide a sales solution that will help your client to be better positioned.

Worthy of note is that all businesses have access to an extensive pool of knowledge - whether this is their understanding of clients' needs and the business environment or the skills and experience of staff. The way a business gathers, shares and exploits this knowledge can be central to its ability to develop successfully. An agile seller uses this information to engage with the client for better understanding of the client's vision/goals/objectives and strategies.

John Hall, CEO and Co-founder, Influence and Co identified 7 ways to identify and evolve with industry trends.

i.   Take advantage of industry research and trends reports.

One of the simplest things you can do to b e t t e r recognize trends is to read research reports or solution guides. Often, industry leaders perform original research and compile their findings in one large report, and by taking the time to actually read through it beyond the executive summary, you can almost always find something in it that's valuable and relevant to what' trending right now in your space. These report usually don't contain the word of god or anything, but reading a variety of reports can help you get a feel for the landscape and where things are headed. And you as an agile seller, can use the information you gather to build a sales pitch helping your client in the right direction.

ii.   Regularly follow publications and influencers in your industry of choice.

In reality, an agile seller, knowing he/she does not have all the time or desire to read through every interesting report an industry leader writes, will make a good alternative making do to read through top blogs and publications in the industry of choice. The agile seller actually takes advantage of information shared through the digital media tools such as LinkedIn to mention just one.

iii. Use different tools and analytics systems to identify the direction trends are heading.

For an agile seller, depending on the industry of choice, the client, the client's goals, and even the size of the company, different tools and metrics will be important for use to identify trends. Personally, when I want information and trends, I use the internet tools to see the bigger picture and also for thought leadership insights. This helps pin point areas for my analysis, after which I usually engage my clients.

iv. Make it a point to surround yourself with smart people.

Agile sellers always surround themselves with smart people confirming the saying, "birds of same feathers flock together" and also the saying "If you're the smartest person in the room, then you're in the wrong room.

v.   Build and maintain a close group of advisers.

Agile sellers always have sponsors or advisers. These are people who guide and mentor them, providing expertise on how best to overcome competition and endearing themselves to clients. This reminds me years ago, while on a sales call, I met a "C" level who intimidated me, till I became speechless. But after I got control over myself and expressed what value I had to offer the "C" level, though he didn't buy anything from me till date, became my sponsor by introducing me to many of his peers through whom I achieved for 3 years running yearly sales target of over 7.5million USD. He helped me see things differently and guided me with the strategy required to be successful in my engagement with other "C" levels. He showed me perspectives to what could influence decisions.

vi.   Ask the right questions, and listen to your clients.

Agile sellers are never afraid to ask current clients what's on their radars (goals/objectives/visions etc) and what they see as future needs in their businesses. This understanding provides important insight into trends which can help develop specific plans for their clients to grow.

vii.   Learn to accept--and even embrace--change.

Agile sellers are quick to accept and adapt, while also embracing change. There are many sellers who is of the opinion that some clients are difficult or stubborn etc., but they fail to understand that they are probably the guilty party who have refused to accept and adapt to the dictates of time with respect to these type of clients. Obviously, if you get too comfortable and adapt to trends too late in the game, a competitor will beat you to the punch. This type of sellers end up playing catch up rather than staying ahead of trends, which causes even more challenges and further distance to sales success. Accepting trends and change as facts of life and embracing them can help you avoid issues.

Whether you're ready for them or not, trends change industries every day. Knowing what's coming around the corner and evolving to meet these client's challenges differentiates you as a modern-day seller aligned to the modern-day buyer providing you with a competitive advantage.

## 4.	Importance of client's Feedback

Feedback is made up of comments by the buyers who you have been engaged with, over a period of time (these could be either in person or as the organization you represent). These feedbacks are considered as indicators for your reputation. Client feedback describes the process of obtaining opinion about either your engagement or your offerings.

Client feedback is so important because it provides sellers with insight that they can use to improve their business overall perception. Listening to your clients' feedback is the only way to guarantee you create an offering they actually want to buy. Clients' feedback is commonly used to review and assess your engagement success. It helps ensure that the clients challenges can/will be resolved.

Improving the client experience should be the primary reason you gather client feedback. The process of winning new business and retaining existing clients is getting harder and harder. Offering an amazing experience that keeps your clients coming back and referring their friends to you is the best way you can stand out from your competition. When you listen to feedback from your client, you tend to create an amazing experience through the questions you ask your clients with regards to what they want. This knowledge and insight will in turn help create a consistent and personalized experience. If you can create an experience that is better than your competitors, your clients will remain loyal and ignore tempting competitive offers. It is that simple. A happy client is a retained client. By feeling your client's pulse through feedback, you enhance the communication between you and the client while keeping your competitors at arm's length. Once again a happy client ensures repeat business.

The feedback you get as a seller is very important as it gives you the ability to build your credibility as an agile seller. Regardless of how you reach out to your clients, your name and reputation as a seller is a brand in itself. It reminds me one of my buyers in one of the big banks who, after several years, moved into a different country in a different continent but still reaches out to me for suggestions on what to do for his company.

It is important to say I have not seen him in well over 10 years, yet he calls me, on the average, every quarter, especially at the beginning of the year during their budgeting. This is a relationship I had built over the years while in active selling.

Agile sellers are best at creating an ambience that meet their clients' needs as they also strive to ensure they exceed the client's expectations. In today's competitive business marketplace, these agile sellers will be the ones that reap strong competitive advantages, have clients' loyalty and trust. Thus, to become an agile seller, I suggest periodic review of the sales process with feedbacks and learn from the experience.

PLAIN

  CLIENT ENGAGEMENT

Sellers must understand what client engagement is all about. Client engagement is a business communication connection between an external stakeholder (consumer) and an organization (company or brand) through various channels of correspondence. This connection can be a reaction, interaction, effect or overall client experience, which takes place online and offline. Client engagement is about encouraging your clients to interact and share in the experiences you create for them as a business and a brand. When executed well, a strong client engagement strategy will foster brand growth and loyalty. Businesses that focus on client engagement are focused on value creation, not revenue extraction. They give people something meaningful beyond a sales pitch: a brilliant end-to-end client experience, great content, or interactive, real-time client support. Burke Alder, a client strategist said: "We need to make our clients' engagement authentic and unique to deliver value daily". He believes in the process in which your organization approaches the management of the client during their journey post sales.

Contemporary smart sellers are advised to be proactive

in their approach knowing that proactive client engagement propels engagement success with the client. Overtime, it has become apparent that the earlier a seller is engaged with the client, the likelihood of sales success as well as the cheaper the engagement process. It is quite simple, this success is a function of a good model based on successful methodology. A good client engagement model needs to be flexible in two key ways: It needs to accommodate different phases of the client lifecycle and it needs to support both scheduled and unscheduled interactions with clients.

Good client engagement models should also help keep you focused on answering the three key questions you need to know about every client:
i.   How is your client measuring value?
ii.   How are they achieving that value?
iii.   How will we provide the right experience that results in trust, loyalty and advocacy?

As an agile seller, your proactive engagement with clients should be governed by an engagement model. A good engagement model helps you understand: a) what the engagement 'moments' are for clients throughout their lifecycle; b) who in your organisation is responsible for interaction with clients at those moments; and c) what the objective or expected outcome is for each of those moments.

In 2008, I studied and researched a company with the goal and vision to build a data centre that can and will accommodate data worth 12 terabytes within the next one year. I researched their operations worked with them for two months to understand the objectives of this vision and then conceptualized a solution which we implemented to meet their objectives after six months of sales engagement. This Data Centre today offers premium data backup and storage service, hosting and disaster recovery services to the public.

Nello Franco (Snr. Vice President, Client Success Talend) belongs to the school of thought of phases in client's engagement. He identified the first key point of an engagement model as the need to work across two very different phases of the client lifecycle, the on boarding phase and the ongoing usage phase.

The first phase, on boarding, is the much higher intensity, much more critical, and much more interactive of the two. Personally, I think of these two phases, you are in closer proximity to the client in the first phase than the second. There is quite a lot during this phase. It is during this phase that more activities happen. This phase requires a high degree of focus. This requirement, carries the workload, intensity and immediate consequences that determine the success of a sale ultimately. Remember once the buyer truly trust you, they will buy from you repeatedly, with minimal cognitive effort. However, before that, you need to persuade them that you can be trusted.

The on boarding phase serves to ensure that your clients are getting off on the right foot and are set up for success with your offerings/solution and creating for the client a logical opportunity for both you and your client to think about, articulate, and agree on how you're going to measure value for the second phase, the ongoing phase.

My suggestions for a confirmation of the first phase include:

i.   Face to face meeting where you both ensure that all sales stake holders meet and identify a face to each other
ii.   Confirmation and profiling of the requirements
iii.   Documentation of these requirements with concrete next steps course of actions

Review of value influence and success stories that will further convince the client to believe in the seller's capability to deliver the required values wanted. In the spirit of Time to Value, it becomes very important that the agile seller moves the process quickly and efficiently as much as possible and that the client momentum is maintained in the process.

Jeff Bezos, CEO of Amazon believes that being obsessed with the client is key to any sales success. This starts with the seller's organisation having a culture which ensures that all stake holders are empowered to provide an amazing clients' experience. I personally believe also that the client experience provided is important to give business owners a way to increase satisfaction, loyalty, and advocacy. It's all about looking at all of your clients and delivering the exceptional service no matter their value. Remember, in the long run, your clients will determine your revenue. It's important to understand that every client wants to be convinced that you truly understand their needs to the point that they also can relate to you on your offerings.

While keeping this momentum, I sincerely do recommend, that once the first phase is defined, you then move seamlessly to measure the time that it will take to progress to the next phase and agree this with your client in the spirit of trust. Then move quickly to analyse the metrics with a deep understanding of any root cause that might create a delay. Going forward, it also becomes imperative that the agile seller, set escalation triggers that will further help and enhance the progression success. All in all you must be proactive to ensure your readiness to becoming your client's advocate for success.

In a nutshell, for the on boarding phase, it is imperative for the agile seller to focus more on the understanding of the client, through active listening, good varying questions, creating a rapport, establishing trust, documenting discussions with exhibition of their values. These all ensure that the client can feel confident that the seller cares about his business.

The second phase, the ongoing phase, however focuses on ensuring that the client achieves the set objectives as identified during the first phase. Identified in this phase are two very important categories namely, the time and event based moments.

Time-based moments are ones that you can put on a calendar, such as a quarterly business review, monthly metrics review, annual account review, or even weekly meetings for your highest of high-touch clients. Time-based moments are great ways to keep your clients interacting with you for the duration of the lifecycle as long as you clearly set expectations and provide valuable feedback to them during those engagement points. If you aren't continuously providing value to your clients during these moments, they'll lose interest and stop attending regular calls/meetings, so be careful not to over-schedule them, and be sure to provide relevant engaging content in each of these engagements.

Event-based moments are ones that are triggered by the occurrence of an event (or non-event in some cases), such as a client logging a high-severity case with your support desk; a new offering release from your company; a change in leadership at your client's; a poor or mediocre survey response; an absence of support cases over a defined period of time; a decrease in overall usage; or a decrease in key usage metrics from a given client. The purpose of event-based triggers is to help you react quickly and appropriately to events that can influence the health of the client relationship – for better or for worse. In either case, the sooner you as the seller reacts to the event that triggered the engagement, the better off you'll become successful with your client.

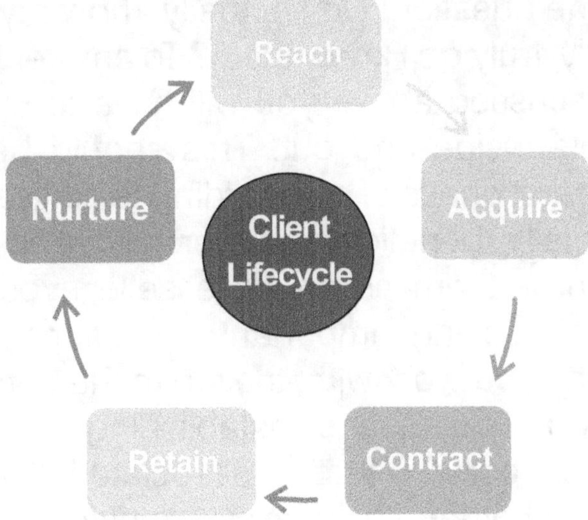

Fig. 4. Engagement trigger.

This model shows some basic engagement opportunities. The agile seller would want to create a model that best fits set goals. Most of all, in a client centric approach, the model should reflect a focus on identifying and supporting the clients' wants, needs, and interests as above.

This book further show case how the knowledge of important events during the ongoing phase will help the seller make a decision how to become the preferred choice with his client, depending on the client and the deal size in question. I will share 3 very important steps that will guarantee you nothing but success with your clients.

First ask the question: Do I actually know my clients? I mean really, truly do I know them? To answer this in line with all discussed above you will have to understand your clients inside and out. This should be the first step in the first phase of on boarding to cultivate a long-term, mutually beneficial partnership. And in order to truly know them as an agile seller, you need to spend time asking important questions of each person that you work with, the top to the bottom in the organization. This means establishing relationships with every person that's associated with your business, whether the decision making level or the influencer level.

I remember a client of mine in 1997-1998, a major bank

in Nigeria, I found myself always spending the evenings with the team to understand the end of day challenges and how best to resolve and improve their efficiency. This I did for 2months and came up with a solution that eventually saw me as their preferred seller. I am sure you know the meaning of being a client's preferred. Same thing I did in 2007 with a buyer interested in building a data centre. I studied their business and came up with a solution after spending lots of time understanding their business needs. Below are some of the questions that really helped me achieve these (there were more, but these readily come to mind now):

i.   What were their teams' goals for the solution within their company?
ii.   What were their personal goals for the proposed solution?
iii.   How were they personally measured and what was their most important KPIs?
iv.   Did they have any alliances or former business relationships with competitors?
v.   What happens if there is no solution?
vi.   What will be the cost impact on the business if no solution?
vii.   What time frame will help ensure the team is seen as efficient?
viii.   Who were the decision makers and the decision making process in the organisation?

Knowing the client through understanding some of the above, helps you understand that which is important to them and the metrics they care most about. However actually applying responses to those metrics, coupled with how you manage and grow the relationship, is just as crucial. It's now your responsibility as an agile seller to customize the relationship, while offering the right solution to what matters most to them. All these will make the client mostly successful. Alan Hall, Forbes says: "whether our sales increases or declines, we should without failure spend quality time with our buyers to understand what's on their minds and respond as quickly as appropriately. It should be crystal clear to all of us that thoroughly knowing and understanding our clients and delivering what they want is the ultimate key to success."

Second, it should be noted that the days of selling are long gone, and most don't want to be sold to anymore. I once met a "C" level buyer who said, "Victor , I only want to communicate with someone who desires my success, that vendor who will help me attain my full potentials, help me solve my needs or solve my problems: are you that seller Victor?" In response, I was speechless for a few minutes and I requested to reschedule the meeting when I could find the answers, because it is the first time I have been asked that question as a seller. It took me two weeks to come up with an answer and when I did, he became one of my favourite buyers for years. We agreed after that session to have a template for supply and only discuss any variance from a cost point of view while others remained constant. This showed me the other side of sales. So as an agile seller the focus should be on the bigger picture with the client and not the immediate sales.

In the words of Mike Myatt Forbes: *"It's not about you, your company, your offerings or your services. It's about meeting client's needs and adding value. When you start paying more attention to your client's needs than your revenue needs, you'll find you no longer have a revenue problem to complain about."*

This is true because "people always buy from people" the news will automatically spread in the industry and your name will be known as an advocate not as a seller. Think of 2 different scenarios. Scenario 1: you walk into a car shop wanting to buy and you are met with the seller who tells you right away the cost of the car and all the functionality of the car; while Scenario 2: you walk into another car shop and met with a seller who starts with what type of car, you want, reason for the choice, what budget you have for the car, etc. Truthfully which of these sellers would you buy from and why…? more so, will you spread the news about that car shop and seller? Your response is as good as mine!

The third and last engagement concept will be to make an agile seller his clients' internal advocate for change. An agile seller is responsible for the relationships with the clients and it is the seller's job to make the clients' business thrive. Since the seller is the owner of the relationship with the client, he is as well responsible for educating them on how to get the most value for their business and how to help them exceed their goals. If they trust you they will open up and share their concerns with you. They will share their experiences within the entire organization, whether positive or negative. The fact is, they also deal with other departments, such as finance and accounting, services, support and likely a few other functions as well. Thus, it is important for an agile seller to understand how they are all interwoven and how they all interact. If you truly gain their confidence and make the clients' success the primary focus, it becomes imperative that you suggest change for your clients for the success of their business.

I have shared my views on how best to systemically engage with your clients in an agile way towards the success of your sales deals. However, There are many ways in which an agile seller can put their clients' first and truly make them look like heroes in their organizations. This should be the ultimate goal. This connotes what my father (HRH. Anthony Alao Femi-Fred Iyelafe II, may his soul RIP) used to say to me whenever I asked him for his opinions. He would share his views and then say: *"there are many routes to the market, the choice of one route lies with you, so choose the effective route".*

PLAIN

CHAPTER 5

SUCCESS CRITERIA FOR AGILE SELLERS (HABIT AND MOTIVATION)

In line with the previous chapter, it is expected from today's business environment that everyone strives to be agile. The pressure to perform and perform fast has become the order of the day using contemporary sales concepts. Sellers are expected to continue to deliver viable, measurable results to the organization in a fast and efficient way, thus necessitating a cursory look at those habits that contemporary sellers require to become successful in an agile way.

I repeat Mark Twain's words that *"Habit is habit and not to be flung out of the window by any man, but coaxed downstairs a step at a time"*. Truthfully we all have habits and these are the things we do without even thinking. It is important to note that good habits can be developed, while bad habits can be tweaked to become good through efforts. The most important thing here is that we should not be discouraged with ourselves because we have not arrived at success, but instead be happy that this weakness has been identified. Along this thought is therefore the need to understand what habits are required to become successful as an agile seller.

Todays' emphasisis on learning and that we should learn and re-learn while sometimes forgetting what we once knew. We should realise that buyers' expectations have changed. Today they want it fast, and they want sellers to add value. Today we are forced to put the bottom line first and above all other things. This, for the buyers, represents understanding.

Today's sellers are needed to make space for more learning especially on agility. Statistics put today's average win rate of deals forecast at about 45% meaning that the other 55% are not aware of things that are going on/in during the sales process. This low percentage is partially attributed to how sellers operate in the new order. Today's sales organizations need to make space for more learning agility. Researchers report that the average win rate of forecast deals is 46 percent. This means 54 percent of time sellers are not aware of things that are going on in the sales process.

This low percentage is partially attributed to how marketing and sales leaders operate in a new work setting. Researchers assert that the brain can go on cruise control. If you are an agile seller, you need to recognize what is required for the new work setting and be prepared with the appropriate learnings. This is the required for effective success with todays' buyers. This is an absolute guarantee to success.

Another school of thought believes that agile practitioners learn to treat failures as valuable learning experiences. They are innovative and creative even when they do not meet their set targets. It is about treasure the wild duck. The phrase "Treasure the Wild Duck" refers to the exploration of ideas that might initially sound strange. This phrase was highlighted as one of IBM core practises considered fundamental to IBM's culture and can be considered as a success pillar for IBM. IBM is a multinational computer technology and IT consulting corporation headquartered in New York, United States. This was conceptualised by Ginni Rometty (the current chairman, president and CEO of IBM), who announced this on the 25th July, 2013 in her podcast.

It is expected that contemporary sellers must seek the root cause, they must always seek to reflect on their buyers' needs/wants and why those needs exist with a very critical appraisal of the buyer's engagement process. They must understand that not only is speed required but with efficiency.

Contemporary sellers must learn to practice and prepare for meetings (be it prospecting/leads or follow up meetings) they must be capable of thinking on their feet. I always suggest to those that ask for my opinion that nothing beats role play amongst sellers. It ensures that all the angles of proposed discussions are addressed before you face your client. As a facilitator, I regularly do lots of role play before my presentations. Sometimes, I practice my opening pitch in front of a mirror knowing that according to global practice, I can lose my audience within the first 3-5minutes. The importance of this I realised in my early facilitation days when my mentor asked me why I was sweating during a presentation. It is now hilarious looking back to those days.

It is quite important that sellers have a role model/sponsor/mentor or guardian in their sales career. The roles of these people cannot be underestimated. You should ask them frequently the "how, why, what and when" questions to fully understand how to be more successful. Personally, my mentors Felix Binggeli and Daniel Cox always help me with this. I never stopped asking them questions to which they always share their opinions, however, they always leave me room to apply my style to my final decision. It is also very important that you ask for their (mentors and coaches) feedbacks for appraisals on how you fared upon sharing their thoughts with you. They (Felix and Daniel) both have had positive influences on me. I remembered once my mentor was presenting to an audience of about 1000 sellers and I noticed how nervous he was.

Despite all praising how well he handled and addressed the delegates, I noticed his nervousness the first few minutes and gave him my feedback to which he was amazed I could pick out. This means feedback is truly food for champions. Upon his resumption back to the stage, he was calm and in control with no sign of nervousness.

Motivation for sellers is equally very important. Contemporary sellers must have a motivation that influence their decisions. These influences also go for today's buyers, thus the need for sellers to understand the "why" behind the buyers' thinking or actions. Because buyers need the sellers, it is therefore important that a seller understands the benefit that the buyer wants even as dynamic as it might be. Need I remind you that "Trust" in business is a very powerful word. Trust raises the questions whether the trust is for your ethics, promise, offering or you as somebody whose words can be taken to the bank. Trust simply put is earned and not requested. Therefore to gain your buyers trust, you must be absolute in all your engagements with the buyer and all around him. Remember when it comes to selling you need to have the motivation to work to the best of your ability with a desire to achieve and channel your energy to that objective.

Highlighting relaxation time for sellers, cannot be underestimated, it is important that you try to take yourself completely out of work mode and do something else that will calm you brain and help you reflect appropriately.

While I was writing this book, an old seller of mine whom I trained on sales skills a year ago, sent me an email thanking me for my guidance as he had used my suggestions and they helped him close almost a million dollar deal. Great news for me, but beyond this it is important to give him the credit he deserves. He simply took ownership and became for me what I call a "self-leader". He had the right mind set and committed to doing everything just about right. He looked at his habits and tweaked them to help him achieve his goal. He simply took control of his time and priorities.

Usually I believe that to become a "self-leader", you must possess these attributes: speak clearly, show confidence, understand the client's wants, articulate a value proposition, address the clients concerns while exhibiting the capabilities to deliver the value requested by the buyer. Remember it's hard to be great on every sales call, but if you can do three things at once: listen intently, respond in real-time with the right answer, and take good notes you will be right on course to success. Becoming a Self-leader is a self-development activity.

To close out this section, I will be reiterating that sellers that switched to an agile sales methodology have been confirmed to see more sales quota achieved and along with that, enjoy a healthy three digits company revenue attainment with over 70 percent of professionals meeting their quota. Sounds too good to be true, right? Yes. Switching to becoming an agile seller comes with lots of benefits. The benefits of an agile sales process are endless, but organizations are often slow to adopt a new framework for selling, despite how critical it is for long term success. We all know from experience how easy it is to get caught up in the quarterly whirlwind and only focus on the fire drill deals that require attention in the here and now. But well prepared sales leaders are adopting agile deal management platforms that will help them not only navigate complex deals today, but plan effectively for many quarters to come.

PLAIN

CHAPTER 6

BUSINESS ACUMEN, UNDERSTANDING THE VALUE

Business acumen is keenness and quickness in understanding and dealing with a "business situation" (risks and opportunities) in a manner that is likely to lead to a good outcome. Additionally, business acumen has emerged as a vehicle for improving financial performance and leadership development.

Business Acumen is a deep and applicable understanding of the system of how a business achieves its goals and objectives. It includes a thorough understanding of the levers that create and position a value proposition to clients and it drives profitability, cash flow, and shareholder value.

S. Anthony Iannarino, believes that business acumen doesn't follow closing, differentiation or prospecting, even though it's on the list. Sellers who may be enabled to close and obtain commitments most of the time do so because of their business acumen. There are lots of ways to differentiate yourself and your company from competitors and business acumen is surely one of the most important. These two attributes and skill sets enable and reinforce each other.

Prospecting is a skill that may precede the need for business acumen, but in most cases it is made immensely more powerful by the addition of business acumen.

What Is Business Acumen? Business acumen is a general understanding of business principles. It is the ability to make thoughtful business decisions. Mostly, business acumen relates to the ability to make decisions that lead to profit. It is only recently that business acumen became one of the primary drivers of success in sales. In the past, it was often enough to possess offering knowledge, features and benefits knowledge, and a strong sales acumen (overcoming objections, rapport building, etc).

A seller seen as having general business acumen is one who consistently exercises sound judgment, the results of his decisions are most often favorable. Those he works with and the client would say he has a quick mind that can assimilate information from many different sources and come up with sound strategic alternatives. He also has the quality of insight, being able to envision what the buyer should do now to bring about a more profitable, successful future.

Successful contemporary sellers understand how business works. They understand their company's go to market strategy, their company's unique value proposition, how they compete and win in their market, and their financial metrics using industry trends as discussed in the earlier chapter. These contemporary sellers are comfortable discussing profitability and financial metrics. They are as comfortable proving ROI while also using the power of one to postulate cost impacts.

Contemporary sellers are comfortable discussing execution with their client's operations staff, and discussing technical ideas and details with their client's technical team. They are more comfortable discussing compliance and legal issues with their client's procurement and risk management teams. They are so on top of their game. They leverage their business acumen to identify areas where value can be created, to build the vision of how that value will solve problems or create a competitive advantage, and to work with their clients to build solutions that deliver the promised outcomes. In short the contemporary seller speaks the business language of the client.

In the past, success in sales depended very heavily on the sellers' sales acumen, but today's buyer has changed all these. I agree with S. Anthony Iannarino when he says: *"while sales acumen is still necessary, business acumen is now equally as important as sales acumen (and in many cases, more!). The business of sales is now the business of business. Contemporary sellers now need the business acumen of a great general manager"*.

We're seeing businesses scale up faster than ever before in history. Worthy of note is Uber. It took Uber 5½ years to sell the first billion rides. However, Uber has a competitor in China, called Didi Chuxing, that took just 11 months to sell their first billion rides — just in China! This is to confirm that no industry anywhere in the today's marketplace is safe. All these are functions of the modern-day buyers. As the market becomes more and more competitive, sellers need to know how to create value and improve business profitability. Anthony Iannarino postulates some important determinants in this regard. Anticipate the future trends (obviously using the Industry trends and analysis as identified earlier in this book). Identify people who impact key business drivers. Thirdly, define key performance metrics.

Identify people who impact key business drivers. Thirdly, define key performance metrics.

All in all, developing stronger business acumen means

more thoughtful analysis, disciplined performance management, paying serious attention to all operational and functional sections of the business with innovative and creative thinking. Also agile sellers with business acumen have the tendency to be mindful of the implications of a choice for all the affected parties coupled with the fact that they are very decisive.

Over the years, I have come to learn that business needs language skills that are critical in this modern era of globalization and cut-throat competition. It is the required skill as a contemporary seller for success. I have tried to identify some of the elements required for business acumen for sellers:

i.   Business Strategy Development and Application
ii.   A Clear Understanding of Financial Acumen
iii.   Tools, Skills, and Concepts of Marketing
iv.   An Understanding of Business Operations.
v.   Business Simulations.

Nevertheless it is never too late to start if you are lacking in the behind from the above. All you have to do is to improve your vocabulary by mastering the specialized words used in business language. Secondly, read lots of business related materials related to your field or industry. Thirdly, learn and understand how to interpret industry trends and analysis. This is not innate, but learned. You can also buttress your skill by watching business oriented programs and listening to lots of business podcasts.

Finally, I recommend lots of practice. Even if you are in the grocery store, practice your learning there. I always say to my delegates, *"if you don't use it, you will lose it"*. You have to grow these competences to the extent that you carry out your organizational strategy with a clear understanding of the industry trends, economic sectors and market dynamics that drive strategic imperatives. It is how well you demonstrate business foresight along with the ability to integrate diverse perspectives.

Business acumen is not only about finance, it is about having a backbone understanding of how decisions will impact profit and growth, thus the need as a contemporary seller to become competent.

I personally think I should differentiate financial acumen from business acumen before I lead you into any confusion. Financial Acumen is believed to be the comprehensive understanding of what drives profitability and cash flow. Profit is the difference between what the business makes from selling offerings (revenue) and how much it costs to produce and sell the offerings (expenses). Jim Collins says: *"Profit is like oxygen, food, water and blood for the body. They are the point of life, and without them, there is no life."* They are the live wire of any business. If profit is the live wire of an organisation, then what is cash? Cash is understood to be the fuel that drives the business; cash equals financial survival for the organisation. Cash and revenue are different. The difference gives rise to Liquidity. Liquidity therefore is how quickly cash can be generated.

Financial acumen also consists of the understanding of budgets, financial statements, key performance measures and how your decisions as a contemporary seller will impact value creation for the buyer.

We also have the need to understand market orientations. This is the deep understanding of the external environment that can influence or impact an organisation and as a seller, you will do well to understand these factors. It includes the ability to analyze and synthesize market and competitive data, while having an understanding of the client's business objectives plus their purchasing criteria.

On the other hand Strategic Perspective paints the overall big picture of understanding of the business route and tools to/for success respectively.

Understanding critical interdependencies across

functions and divisions, and grasping the short- and long-term trade-offs of business decisions is a skill that must be learned so as to be able to articulate the right value proposition to the client as a contemporary seller

.

We have been looking at the basics of being a successful seller through contemporary and agile capabilities. Now let's take a moment to reflect on the importance of this knowledge.

Importance of understanding the key drivers of business and using them to make good things happen means: seeing the "big picture" of your client's organization, understanding the importance of communications, using your knowledge to make good and informed decisions, understanding how your actions impact your client's key performance measures, and effectively communicating your ideas to your clients on what they stand to gain with your offerings/value proposition. Having said all these, you, as the contemporary seller, stands to gain the appreciation of top management's strategic decision makers.

With the current trend of achieving targets, while equipped with new information technology in this digital age, it has become easier for sellers to become myopically immersed in their own objectives failing to align with the client's. This immersion can have the effect of obscuring their view of the client's bigger picture. This may lead to the lack of motivation to invest personal energy in the client's business operations.

Sellers that engage in developing a good business acumen are called agile sellers as they provide a clearer vision and an overall context within which buyers can be more effective and efficient. They are motivated and are likely to be innovative in their engagement with the client. This engagement goes a long way to impact the ultimate bottom line results. . In a nutshell,they start thinking like business owners. Aligning with Jill Konrath who says: *"You're dealing with educated people who want conversations and collaboration, not pitches of any sort."* It thus become imperative thatsellers align with the buyer and his business needs.

PLAIN

    # NEEDS BASED SELLING

This book is intended to help bring you up to speed with the needs of todays' buyers. I personally feel that the ability to implement the Need Based Selling approach which represents "Putting the customer first" lies at the core of every successful sales interaction. It becomes paramount to understand the key concepts of this thoughts. Nick Kane firmly identified three different tactics of putting the client first. He identified the importance of not wasting your client's time; addressing your clients priorities and not yours the seller; and lastly, get really good at confirming your client's needs.

Contemporary sellers attempt to be an "assistant buyer" where the client see's you as trusted, this is much better than merely breaking down the client's resistance through brute force. This approach is typically referred to as consultative or needs-based selling, because it focuses on identifying and fulfilling the customer's needs.

Gone are the days of conventional selling despite the appealing logical structure. Gone are those days of features of an offerings, (FAB), Features, Advantages and Benefits we discussed earlier. Today's marketplace calls for agility, where sellers are encouraged to ask open-ended questions which have become the central skill required for needs-based selling. This, when used skilfully, will always remain the best effective sales technique in many situations. I therefore suggest that you as a seller should endeavour to ask open questions. Open questions help define buyer's needs, helps alter or position your offerings to address those needs, thereafter raising the value to the customer and the likelihood of offering engagement.

Let's look at this example. A buyer interested in cloud based offering meets with a seller and says I need a proposal for cloud offering: a conventional seller will all but get excited and proceed with putting a proposal together, while on the other hand, the modern day seller will endeavour to understand the drivers for this need through questions to the buyer. Potential questions could be, "what is informing this decision", "what are the expected end goal to this decision", "what could possibly happen if this does not happen", "how is the client currently running his operations with the cloud", etc. These open questions is to further help the seller understand the buyers' business, business process and the business goals. These types of questions will endear the buyer towards becoming a trusted advisor rather than just as a vendor. Noting that these questions will help determine the actual need of the buyer with accurate assessment of the need. This is my suggestions to this potential type of opportunities.

Identifying how not to waste your client's time, you must come to terms that today's buyers are more informed than ever before. They have all the digital tools to be informed, thus they do not need any reason to be ignorant, I suggest that your time with them should be about listening to understand and identify that which they don't know so you can add value to your engagement with them. Worthy of note is that there are still quite a lot of other clients who rely heavily on what you have to share with them, but again the key is about listening to their needs. This gains you the role of a trusted advisor and being a trusted advisor gives you the competitive edge with your clients.

To address your client's priorities and not yours, you as an agile seller must be learned and equipped with good questioning skills that will help you further understand the client's needs/priorities as well as impacts. You must understand what drivers (discussed in the last chapter) drives your clients and how you can best mitigate against these. What compelling risk they (your clients') are exposed to with their challenge. Remember questioning and listening are key to help you address your client's needs and priorities.

Thirdly, as a follow up to the above, questioning and listening not only help you gain trust, but you must always ensure you confirm client's responses during your client's engagement. As much as this gives you added credibility for active listening I however, do caution against irritative confirmation of every sentence during discussion. This is absolutely the best time for agile sellers to use the 80/20 client engagement rule for the right professional balance. This will further enhance the confidence reposed on you as their trusted advisor, which again shows that you care about them and their business not just the sale at stake. This will lead to repeat engagements.

I believe that to succeed in sales today you must be equipped with agile sales skills required to understanding and performing core sales strategies/ tactics while also adhering to a proven methodology that focuses on solving client's challenges. It is also very important to identify the appropriate stake holders and the buying process that enhances the needs based approach.

What are Needs-oriented questioning: Agile sellers understand that asking questions remains the only effective key to becoming trusted because it's the only way to uncover your customer's needs. Every worthwhile relationship you build and valuable piece of new business you win comes down to your ability to ask questions (not just questions, but the right questions). I again re-iterate that only by asking the right questions are you truly able to understand the client and how you can help them. This differentiates you as an agile seller as this demonstrates your focus on your client. By asking these openquestions you are telling your client that his or her needs are your primary concern. These types of questions include phrases such as; "tell me more", "help me understand", "describe your current operations", "in the immediate to short term, how do you plan to?"

In contrast to the above, we also have Offering-Oriented Questions. These deal directly with offerings or services. This focuses on you as the seller rather than the buyer. It is myopic for continuity selling. These questions focus on your need to sell rather than the buyer. Types of questions are inclusive of phrases such as "my offering can do", "we have lots of this offerings", "working with my offerings, you stand to benefit more", etc.

It is important for sellers to note that Needs-oriented questions keep the clients' involved in the sales process giving the buyers a feeling of control. This also presents sellers with the opportunity to explore and uncover further needs. There are, however, two types of these

The other type of need is the Target Level. The target level needs are only uncovered when the right questions are asked. To achieve a comprehensive understanding, it is expected that you as the agile seller dig a little further, using well-structured needs-oriented questions, which will uncover additional needs. An example of this could be from asking follow up questions to the initial view of the buyer. A client says: "this year I need to reduce my operational cost";an ideal follow up question should be in the range of "by how much", "by when", "what happens if this KPI is not met", what initiatives do you have in place to making this happen" etc. Below a pictorial view of what a Sales Iceberg looks like.

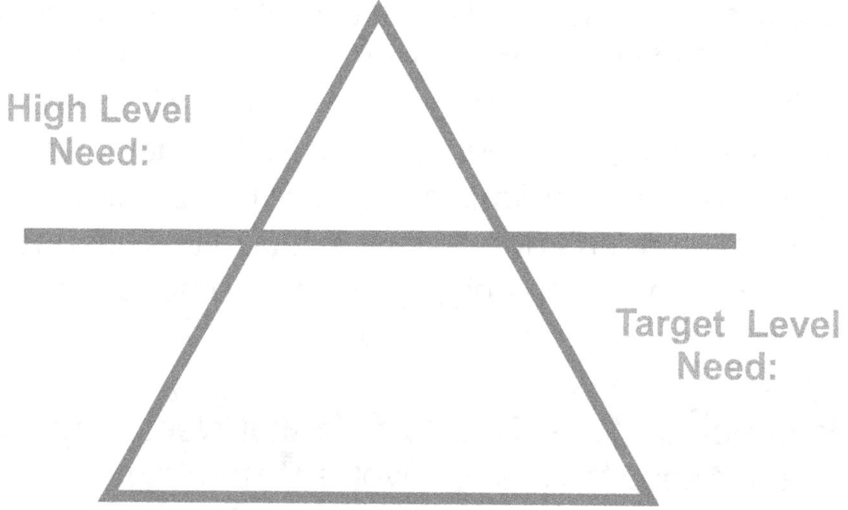

Fig. 5. Sales Iceberg

Target Level Needs

Like an iceberg where most of the ice is underwater, target level needs aren't always obvious. Target Level Needs need to be sought out, explored and prioritised.

The next time you're with a customer and discussing a product group ask a needs-oriented question. That is, a question that's not product focussed but aimed at uncovering needs for specific offerings. This is the essence of needs based selling.

1.   SET THE AGENDA

It is essential that any sales call begin with an agenda. Whether it is an existing client or a potential new one, the sales professional should state an agenda. It is only professional courtesy to address the client's question of "why the client should sacrifice his time for the seller". There is the acronym W. I. I. F. M. (What Is In It For Me). This means the client is curious to know what the stakes are from the seller, thus a good standard opening is, "Mr. client, what I'd like to do today is to first talk about you - ask a few questions about your business and find out what is happening with you, help me understand what you do and the potential objectives of your job roles etc. Further agenda statements could be along the lines of "tell me more about what you do, what is happening at the company, and then the client can thereafter determine whether there is a reason to work together. How does that sound?" The key here is to get agreement from the client to continue the sales call. Once the client agrees, then next step will be the needs analysis or questioning stage.

2. NEEDS ANALYSIS

This phase is usually considered as the engage phase where asking questions about the client's business should be a conversation where the seller ensures that the client gets to talk more. This phase usually is characterized as the body of the whole engagement process. Here is when the seller uses his/her two ears and one mouth in equal proportion. This is where the 80/20 principle comes into play. Good listening skills that we did talk about earlier in this book comes to the fore. Active listening is very important in any sales call, most especially in this engagement phase where the client gets to reveal lots information about themselves and their business based on the quality of the questions. It is critical that the seller NOT TRY TO SELL during the needs analysis, but rather listen more and in-between the lines of things said by the client. Resisting the urge to sell may be difficult for some sellers, but the structural order that was set at the beginning must be followed, and here we are letting the client tell us about them. The goal of Need analysis is to uncover problems, concerns, or issues that the client is having.

Again, no selling should occur before the client's needs are uncovered. When needs or concerns are identified, the next step is to qualify or determine how important or critical the issue is to the client. Ask the client what it would mean to the business if the   situation they identified could be corrected. If they respond with emotion or with great interest in how that could be accomplished, the seller who can provide a solution will most likely get the sale. If the issue is not that important or if the client is not seeing the situation as a pressing issue, then it does not qualify as a need and should not be pursued as an opportunity. Once the pressing need or needs are identified, a good question to ask the client is, "can you and I agree to work together on finding a solution to this (or these) concerns?" The answer to this question will determine the level of buy in and interest from the client. This phase is also known as the refining phase where questions on some fundamentals sales concepts are addressed. These concepts is built around B. A. N. T. (Budget, Authority, Need & Timelines).

Budget is very important to understand who owns and will deploy the allocated financial resources. This also helps to understand if it is within the client's priority list for execution. Authority helps identify the decision makers, influencers and possibly sponsors for the identified opportunity. Need I believe is self-explanatory on its own, while Timeline will help identify not only the priority rating for the opportunity, but also within what timeframe the opportunity is currently being considered.

3.   **SUMMARIZE**

When the client is finished telling about themselves and their business, there would have been either one or more needs uncovered. Professionally, it is expected that a summary recapping the highlights of the earlier engage phase articulated to show that the seller truly listened and focussed on the client. Unfortunately, this is the phase where most sellers are so much in a hurry that they forget or ignore. Unfortunately, ignoring or forgetting to recap highlights could mean, lack of interest to the client or that the seller displayed an act of selfishness to want the client's money and nit the client's interest. It is a delicate balance needed during this phase of engagement. The end result of guilty at this phase is that you leave the door open to competition to finish the job for you after all the efforts being put in. I therefore personally urge readers of this book to pay attention to a summary of the engagement phase for effective understanding of discussions thereby avoiding any contradictions or wishful hearings.

By recapping or summarizing what those needs were, the client will know that they were listened to and will give the seller more credibility because they heard and understood what was said. Also, by gaining agreement from the client that these needs exist, the seller can begin to plan a recommendation to answer the needs or solve the problem.

4.   TRANSITION

After the needs are revealed and agreed upon by the client, the sales professional should set the table for the recommendation step. The recommendation phase is also known as the influencing phase where the seller is expected t o showcase value with an appropriate proposal of moving forward. This proposal is not the type of wedding proposal, but a proposal of value. An example here could be proposing a workshop to further showcase what the offering value presents to the client. In this phase, the seller could also propose a site visit, event attendance, reference call with another client who has implemented a similar project to success. My favourite during my days was always a workshop. The reason for my choice of workshop was to help me meet other stake holders involved with the opportunity so I can identify more support/sponsors from within the clients organization. If however, this phase will involve a second sales call, set up the next appointment where specific plans to solve the concerns will be revealed and a recommendation made assertively. An easy way to do this could be to say,"if I had a way to help your business resolve this issue, would you be interested in hearing about it?" If the client says yes, you are on the way to a sale! This phase usually ends with a closed question to the client leading the client to either a "Yes or No". If Yes then progress has being made, but if otherwise, then a repeat is required knowing there are missing links during the engagement phase. More of this is addressed in my next chapter handling objections if it's the case.

5. RECOMMENDATION

Based on the needs that were uncovered, the recommendation can be prepared and delivered as value proposition. If the client has agreed that the need is there, and if your offering will solve the issue, concerns or objectives, then closing the sale will have a higher probability.

PLAIN

    # HANDLING OBJECTIONS

would be doing a dis-service to sellers if I do not share my thoughts on potential deal stoppers known as Objections. The toughest aspect of any sales position is overcoming a buyer's objections. Objections are roadblocks, distractions, obstacles & potential deal stoppers. The seller's goal is to have a convincing response to these road blocks. As many experienced sellers know, almost all sales calls are met with at least one objection. Most times sellers are ignorant of these objections and they pass them by ignoring them or sometimes even defend them which will ultimately yield no result.

Objection handling means responding to the buyer in a way that changes their mind or alleviate their concerns. Handling sales objections is by addressing your buyer's concerns about your offerings in order to create a personal buy-in.It is one of the stages where the seller, during the sales process will have to address the objections and resistance from the buyer. It is not the time to argue because there are differences, but rather it should be seen as an opportunity to progress the sale. I consider this another opportunity to further demonstrate and explain more about the value offered.

Let us look at this example where a child staying with someone else other than his/her parents feels homesick and says he/she wants to go home. objection, "I want to go home": the adult shows understanding with an empathy responding with "oh ok, I acknowledge how you feel about going home and being home sick": test "If I were in your shoes, I will feel the same way": Addressing the objection, "but you know if we have some rest now, then we will have renewed energy to walk home tomorrow": validating the objection with a closed question, "will it be ok to sleep now and get some rest for tomorrow": your guess on the understanding and response of the child's feeling after this exchange is as good as mine.

Hearing the response "no" is usually not pleasant, but look at it this way, if all answers to a sale was yes, would there be a need for sellers. I am sure it will definitely be a no and then we will have no job. Rejection is what we all struggle with and how we surmount this determines how professional we are in our sales career. Rejection provides additional opportunity for deal closure, providing sellers further opportunities to differentiate themselves, it is most times an indication of interest from the buyer. Leonardo Da Vinci says: *"It is easier to resist at the beginning than at the end."* Experience has shown that most sellers will receive a "no" at the start of an engagement most often than during the engagement phase of the sales cycle. This is usually the best time to put up a great attitude to give time, attention and added credibility.

Objection handling requires a deep understanding of the root cause of the objection and below are some of the potential objections from buyers (there are more though, but these readily come to mind): These objections are road blockers to potential sales, they are potential deal stoppers. They cause and create panic to sellers.

i.   Cost of offering (e.g. offerings too expensive etc.)
ii. Extra features add on (e.g. want of dashboard at every level for a software opportunity etc.)
iii. Project priority (e.g. this project is not in my priority etc.)
iv. Budget constraint (e.g. there is no budget availability etc.)
v.   Meeting Timing (e.g. I have a busy schedule at the moment etc.)
vi. Gatekeepers (e.g. I have a different seller in mind etc.)
vii. Delivery competency (e.g. I am not convinced of your delivery capabilities etc.)
viii. Project manager (e.g. Your project manager lacks depth etc.)

Some sellers argue with their buyers or try to pressure

them into backing down, however, this is not a true way for objection handling. Instead of telling the buyer they're wrong, help them come to a different conclusion of their own accord. And if you can't persuade them, then you have to accept and strive to maintain the relationship.

Handling objections, however does requires sellers' rap attention at identifying an objection during engagement with the buyer. I have had quite a few in my time. I once had a buyer who showed interest in the offering, but was not convinced that my organisation could provide post implementation support service. Upon further dialogue I uncovered their preference was to have a support service included for 8 hours per day 5 days a week for the first year. This was because they were still not sure of the stability and success of the solution I was offering. I acknowledged their concern and asked further questions that led to another workshop with an increased scope of work (meaning more money) and we closed the sale with all parties happy. Today the rest is history. It is how well you address a buyer's concern rather than defending a concern. This shows a difference.

Objections in the sales process can be professionally handled through different ways some I am highlighting below:

i. Listen Fully to the Objection: To identify an objection, you have to first and foremost hear the objection to identify that it's an objection. Objection is considered an obstruction to the progression of an engagement. Your first reaction when you hear an objection may be to jump right in and respond immediately. I suggest you resist that urge and not make any assumption, but rather take the time to listen to the objection fully and ask follow up questions to understand the root cause. It is not the time to react defensively, but rather show apt attention to the buyer that you are listening and interested to understand why the objection. Listening means you have noticed the objection and heard the client. An example *"your offering is too expensive"* says the buyer. The seller should acknowledge by accepting the seller do have a valid point, but then, should ask, *"why does the buyer feel the offering is expensive"* because there could be different reasons for this perception. It could be budget or other projects are in the topmost priorities to be included in the buyers budget at the moment. I suggest always why. If effectively found, then you know you are on the same page of engagement and be ready to move on to the next phase of understanding the objection.

ii.   Understand the Objection Completely:
      Experience has shown over time that objections
      hide the underlying issues for most part of the
      time. I suggest you see this as an opportunity to
      understand why is the objection an issue for the
      buyer, why the buyer is bringing this up, what can
      be done to mitigate this concern. It is important
      that the concern is acknowledged with
      thoughtfulness for a moment though and then
      repeat to the buyer to confirm with the buyer you
      heard what "his/her" concern is.

iii. Acknowledge the objection: Acknowledging the
      buyer's objection means it's time for you to
      confirm your understanding of the buyer's
      concern. This is where you have to show empathy
      for the concern. Acknowledging a concern is
      considered as reassuring signal about your
      attitude as a seller towards addressing the buyers
      concern. Your acknowledgement signals that
      you are listening with respect. This is where I
      suggest the seller takes the opportunity to further
      get collaborative in the engagement with
      qualifying questions to uncover the underlying
      issues behind the concerns. I would like to
      emphasise here that acknowledging an
      objection is not the same as agreeing, but rather
      to validate the concern. The caution here is neither

to be rebuttal, but rather to be collaborative or use the generic acknowledgements. Empathise with the buyer showing you care and you are listening to his concern. An example could be using phrases like *"I hear this a lot, I am sorry you feel that way, it must really be unpleasant for you, I hear what you are saying, etc."* *it all depends on the circumstances of the engagement.*

iv.   Respond Properly: To respond properly to an objection, you would require tact in recognizing that mental aspects of the concern. Effective response determines the final direction of the sale, thus the need for a cautious influence response to progress your engagement. An example of this for a frequent concern on price from the buyer could be: *Buyer: "your offering is too expensive as much as I am interested, its way off the roof": Seller: I hear what you are saying, however, how would you suggest we address this together. This positive response will further open up more collaborative engagement. The seller could also respond, "yes, I understand, price is always the issue."* there are lots of ways to respond, but the seller must recognize that the opportunity to progress his engagement is now. Here is the time to best demonstrate your uniqueness, to make yourself the differentiator, the catalyst, why you are different from competition with the values you bring to the table etc. I suggest you as the seller seizes the opportunity to help the buyer become a star, make them feel comfortable on this journey with you.

v. Confirm objection satisfaction: Confirming the buyer's satisfaction by assessing their response provides you with their feedback that you've been successful in handling the objection. For example, *"Have I addressed your concern to your satisfaction?" or "Does this make more sense now?"* the confirmation phase is usually characterised with closed question that helps determine the final outcome whether it is a "go or no go". This step ensures you did address and handled the buyer's concern and can progress your engagement.

While sales objections are rarely great news, they can indicate that the buyer has an interest in your offerings; objections most times presents an opportunity. By being proactive and attempting to work with the buyer to overcome his concerns, you can create a great foundation for a long-term relationship based on meeting the buyer's needs.

Daniel Cox, (my role model) a strategist negotiator,

once used a phrase I fell in love with. This I share with my readers so they can also see positives from client's objections. The phrase, I call the three Fs (Feel, Felt & Found) provides a very good baseline to a good objection handling. He says: first step is to listen, this is as important as acknowledging with empathy before you clarify the buyer's concerns. This will go a long way to ease the concerns of the buyer, an example could be "I acknowledge how you feel on this", you are not alone with this feeling, others have felt same way, however, what they eventually found out was….". Then the value offered. I urge you to read in between the lines on how the words "feel, felt & found" were used as appropriate and in the context of the engagement.

If however, otherwise after handling the objections, you still loose the deal, here are potential ways to go about it in readiness for another day.

i.   Don't take it personally. Usually, a rejection in sales could mean either, your offering wasn't what the buyer needed or there was a misunderstanding during engagement.
ii.   Expect it. Rejection does happen, but there is always another day.
iii.   Be professional. You need to remain polite and extremely professional.
iv.   Ask why the loss, to be prepared for the next time.

v.   Talk with your teammates, treat it as a necessary step.

vi.   Be persistent.

BOOK REVIEW

The ability to share one's thoughts and knowledge successfully around a specific topic is a gift. My friend Victor - you have excelled in this through your book.

Many years of sharing and coaching hundreds to thousands of his own sellers, Victor has produced a book which I think will add value to many sellers lives. In one chapter he discusses the value of being well presented - Victor - you are the epitome of sales "classiness". I see this quality in both your passion for the skill as well as in your passion and desire to ensure your students (of sales) become the best they can possibly be.

I sincerely hope this is only the first book in a series of many. To the future readers of this book - read the words in this book and know that they will help you close those deals, they will help you be the best seller you could possibly be, they will surely make you stop and think and most of all they will most definitely ensure your job in sales is a passion and not merely a job.

To Victor Femi-Fred you have excelled in your

endeavours and to all future readers of Contemporary Smart Selling, keep the book close, make many notes and as Victor has so wisely mentioned – "you have two ears and one mouth" - use them in that proportion. Sales is sexy - go out and make lots of money.

Michele Kruse
Global Client Manager at Insights
Lincoln, United Kingdom

The way people buy has changed massively recently with the advent of the internet and online shopping. Today's buyers have much more information at their fingertips and the role of the Seller has had to change too. We can no longer rely on providing information on our products; we now need to understand the client's challenges, and ideally leave with them with some new insights after having interacted with the buyers.

Victor in his book Contemporary Smart Selling highlights some of the changes that have taken place and shows ways sellers can go about to address them to stay current in this new world. Definitely worth adding to your "sharpening the saw" library to stay current and relevant. Great job victor.

Felix Binggeli
IBM GSS Learning Leader for Growth Markets,
Sales Learning for Central Eastern Europe Middle East Africa, Austria

Victor, I consider you as one of the rarest gift God gave to me and our meetings have always been blessed. Many surprises from you, and the writer in you never let my expectations flag down.

Summary of what I enjoyed reading your book: Your vision, your mission and your purpose to put into being is so evident and worth exploring. I understand this comes from all your sales and delivery expertise, from the hundreds to thousands of professional you have met and coached. The 'target' audience this book caters ranges from young to the most experienced sellers, and the book drives through their minds and hearts towards success. Competitors in the book are not 'visible' ones alone, but, also the invisible self and their instincts. Human is the biggest factor that differentiates you from the machine, in the near future. So overwhelming to see the articulation of how human behaviors matter in this book.
Victor in this book addresses all the aspects described above with all the required ingredients. Sales is more 'impactful' only when you set your pace and stage. How much more can we ask for?

Denny Jose
ASEA Pacific IBM Sales Learning Consultant and Facilitator